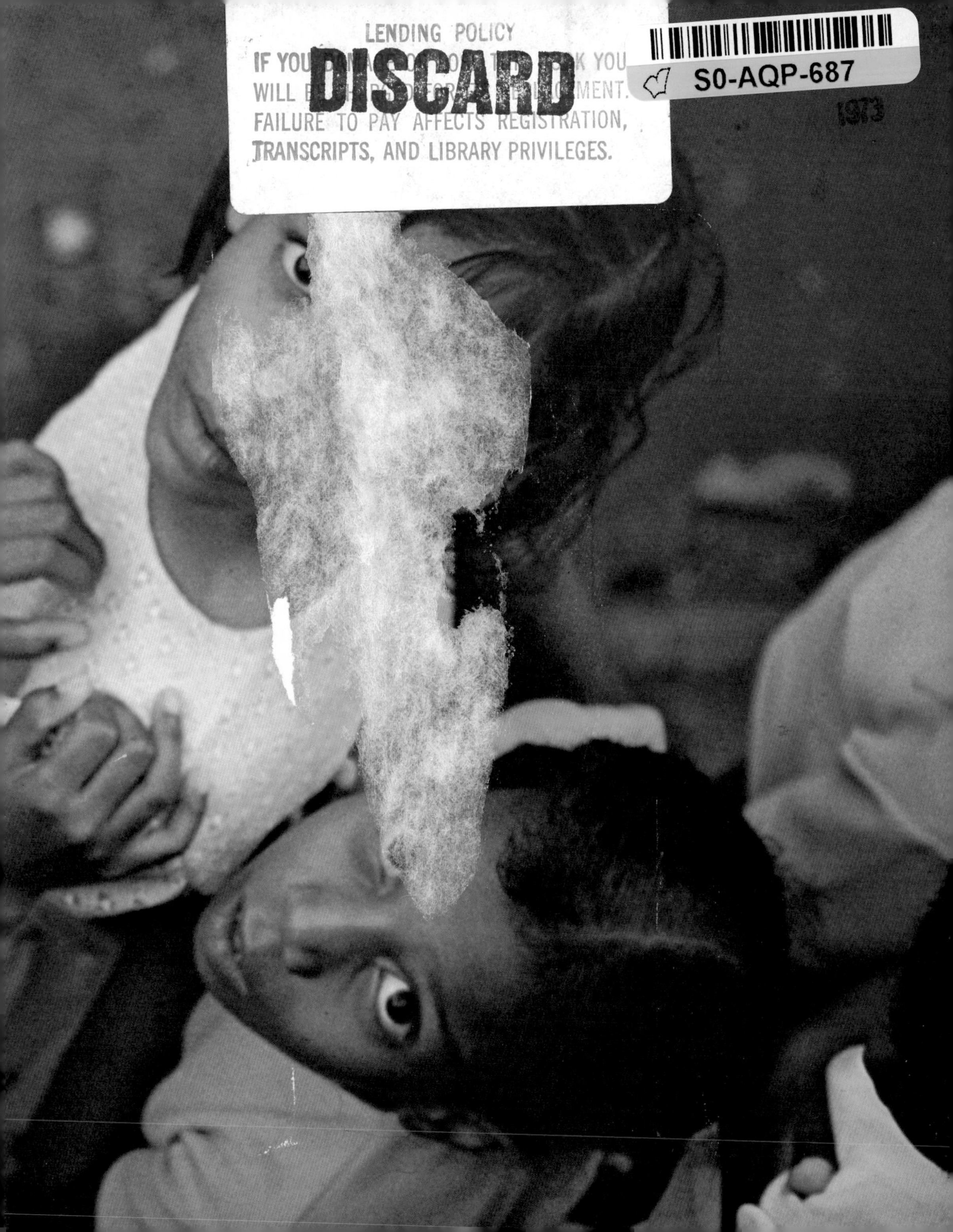

marti

nique

photography by bernard hermann
les éditions du pacifique
hachette antilles

summary

history

The first occupants of Martinique, the Arawaks, were conquered by the Carribeans. Columbus discovered the island in 1502. It became a French possession in 1635. The English subsequently occupied it three times. Schoelcher abolished slavery in 1848. (*page 8*)

market places

The market places are a profusion of shapes, colors and smells emanating from the lush variety of flowers, fruit, vegetables and fish — all part of the exotic and abundant tropical flora and fauna. (*page 25*)

carnival

The Carnival — *Vaval* — four hectic days of uninterrupted celebrations: from Sunday to Wednesday, each day a pretext for wearing a different costume. Fort-de-France lives at an exhilarating and exhausting rhythm as people swarm through the streets until the whole island seems transformed into one immense crowd of dancers. (*page 18*)

fort-de-france

A simple fortress built in the marshes, Fort-Royal became, in 1682, the capital of Martinique. Named Fort-Republique in 1793, known as Fort-de-France since 1808, the town now comprises almost one-third of the population of the island. (*page 14*)

population

More than 300,000 Martiniquans live in about 400 square miles, and over 50% of the population is less than 20 years of age. History has made Martinique a veritable melting pot which has given rise to an original and beautiful race of people. (*page 21*)

traditions

The creole soul is composed of a mixture of traditions, superstitions and customs which gives Martinique a very distinct atmosphere, reflected in the language, folklore and beliefs, as well as in the music and dancing. (*page 76*)

saint-pierre

Saint-Pierre was the most prosperous and lively town of Martinique, and indeed of all the West Indies, in the eighteenth century. In 1902, the volcano of Mount Pelée erupted and completely destroyed the town. (*page 37*)

cock-fighting

This traditional sport is practised throughout the West Indies. Behind the obvious cruelty of the pastime which, like bullfighting, has many fanatics and opponents, cockfighting embraces a kind of social rite which often serves as a pretext for meetings, gambling and oratory contests. (*page 98*)

sugar cane

Although it is not the only resource of the island, sugar cane plays the principal role in the economy and provides employment for 40,000 people during the cutting season, which lasts for three months. Besides sugar refining, Martinique is renowned for the highest quality rum produced in the region. (*page 42*)

canoe races

The traditional *gommiers* — canoes made from a species of gum tree — are now rare. Boat races always feature on the program of festivities for celebrating the day of the patron saint of each village, but nowadays the islanders usually race locally-made yawls. This sport requires well-built boats, powerful crews and large crowds of supporters. (*page 90*)

fishing

The people of Martinique learned from their Carribean neighbours the science of navigation, as well as fishing techniques. Although there are only about 3000 professional fishermen, almost every Martiniquan fishes as a pastime, using a wide array of traps, lines and nets, both inside the reefs as well as in the open sea. (*page 105*)

97527

the west indies

The appropriate French name Antilles (ante-islands, ante-isles) indicates that these are the first landmarks sighted when sailing from Europe, bound for the American continent.

About 3,000 miles from Africa and 4,000 miles from Europe, the West Indies are strung out in a huge semi-circle stretching from Florida to the north-east coast of South America. They are divided into two distinct geographical groups, known as the Greater and the Lesser Antilles, and these groups are further fragmented into a myriad of islands and islets. Whilst differing greatly in size and political structure, the French writer, A. Césaire, aptly described them as "*terriblement unes; unes par la nature, unes par les conditions economiques et sociales unes par le peuplement*".

a multitude

The Antilles, geographically situated between the Atlantic Ocean and the Carribean Sea, comprise an infinite number of islands and islets, varying in size from 110,000 square kilometers (Cuba) to 13 squa kilometers (Saba). The political structures and form of government are equal diverse and often antagonisti There are seven types government, two radical opposite economic system and at least four language Some islands are British, som French, and some Dutc while others are independen but under the areas of infl ence of the Great Power Certain islands have rigid tot itarian regimes, while othe are fervently marxist.

a strange partition

In the sixteenth century, t

uropean powers began to :plore that part of the globe :therto marked "*terra in-gnito*". The archipelago of e West Indies rapidly ·came the battleground for .eir rivalries, and the area was vided and subdivided into most as many trading posts there are islands. In the ·enzied rush for supremacy, .e great maritime powers me and time again conquer-l, lost and reconquered the fferent groups, individual lands, and even parts of olated islets. (In 1804 Great ritain even installed a gar-son of 200 soldiers on the nely Diamond Rock, situat-l only a mile or so from the ast of Martinique).

he islands of the West Indies id their riches often served as iwns to settle accounts after e conflicts between Euro-an rivals. (Louis XV prefer-d to give up a "few acres of ow" in Canada, as he called , rather than cede Martini-ie, the island of sugar). This irtering and the incessant ianges of sovereignty con-iued until the nineteenth ntury, when the map of the est Indies began to take its esent shape, and the parti-on became more or less cepted.

nited west indies?

ie twentieth century is the ne for reappraisal of the aps formerly drawn by ilonial conquerors as the est Indians search for their dependence, economic development and polital unity. But those who speak of the Antilles as a whole tend to see only the similarity of climate, scenery and race, whilst omitting to take into account the physical peculiarities of each place, and especially the historical facts or accidents which have led each one of the islands to their present situation.

Just as the climate or the scenery cannot be categorically divided into wet and dry seasons, or tropical forest and desert, the populations of the different areas, as a result of living for generations under a variety of conditions, have evolved many forms of social structure.

Throughout the region, there have been three elements of population — Indians, Europeans and Negroes. The evolution, from a racial point of view, has been almost identical: the almost total disappearance of the Indians, the implantation of relatively few white settlers, and the importation of large numbers of African negroes. In each island, unique measures have been applied to the problems of racial stratification, of colonization and of slavery.

Certain islands, such as Haiti, freed themselves of their colonial past as early as the beginning of the nineteenth century, whilst others, like Cuba, overthrew the original structure only in the middle of the twentieth century. Some areas chose mutiny as the means, others revolution, while yet others managed to alter the structure in a peaceful and democratic way. (The latter include the formerly British West Indies, which are now independent, and the French Antilles, where the populations chose to become departments of France). Such a diversity of results and procedures, added to the obstacles of language, mentality and economic resources, make it easy to understand why it is utopian today to hope for or dream of a "complete revision of the political structure of the Antilles" (A. Césaire).

the french antilles

Separated from France by 7,000 kilometers of ocean, Guadeloupe with its dependencies (part of Saint-Martin, Saint-Barthélemy, Marie-Galante, the Saints and Désirade) plus Martinique, form a group with a distinct personality — the French West Indies.

Parts of the Lesser Antilles, they are considered to be an integral part of France, while the Windward Islands, Martinique and Guadeloupe, the largest in area, are departments.

a privileged island

"The eyes are dazzled by the splendour that one could scarcely dream of. This tropical Nature, revealing all its beauty, is truly that whi inspires so many poets. Ea ray is resplendent in powerf harmony. One feels, one se all that Nature has done f these privileged isles".

The twentieth century trav ler would not describe t island in the same way Rear-Admiral Aube did wh he discovered it in 1882.

Tourist brochures, the cinem magazines and advertisemer have acquainted the who world with these most beau ful of islands and their m nificent scenery. Airli companies today offer to ta you where yesterday you on dreamed of going, but of tropical places and of all t islands on earth, sure Martinique ranks as the mc privileged of these privileg islands.

Martinique has an area 1,080 square kilometers. It 65 kilometers long and kilometers across at the wid part.

Amongst the wild disarray the tropical forest in t north, exotic tree-ferns, lian epiphytic plants, moss a flowers compete with o another to climb the footh of Mount Pelée (1,397 m.) a the Pitons du Carbet.

An evenly distributed rainf abundantly irrigates the ent island.

The tropical climate is equat with slight variations at high altitudes and as a result varying wind conditions.

Sea temperatures range fro

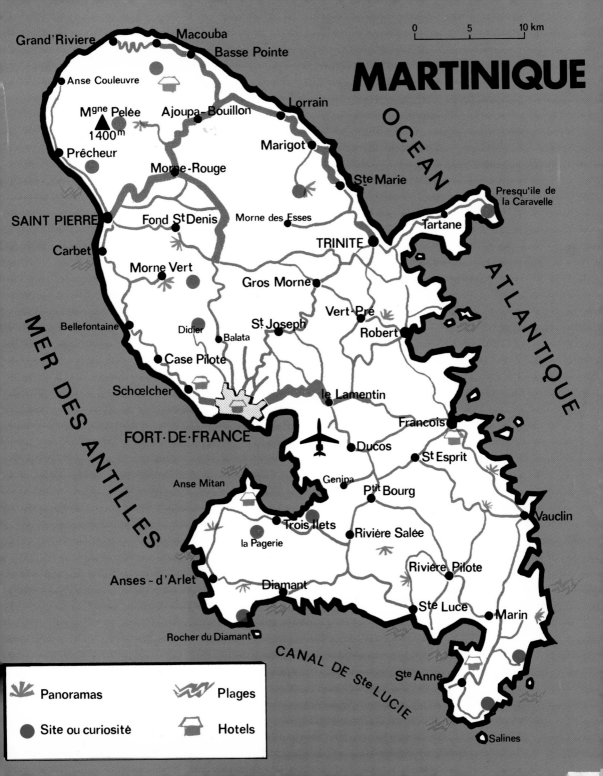

MARTINIQUE

0   5   10 km

OCEAN

ATLANTIQUE

MER DES ANTILLES

Grand'Riviere
Macouba
Basse Pointe
Anse Couleuvre
Lorrain
M^{gne} Pelée
1400^m
Ajoupa-Bouillon
Prêcheur
Marigot
Morne-Rouge
Ste Marie
SAINT PIERRE
Fond St Denis
Morne des Esses
Tartane
Presqu'ile de la Caravelle
Carbet
TRINITE
Morne Vert
Gros Morne
Bellefontaine
Didier
Balata
St Joseph
Vert-Pré
Robert
Case Pilote
Schœlcher
le Lamentin
FORT·DE·FRANCE
Francois
Ducos
St Esprit
Anse Mitan
Genipa
P^{tit} Bourg
Vauclin
Trois Ilets
la Pagerie
Rivière Salée
Anses - d'Arlet
Rivière Pilote
Diamant
Ste Luce
Marin
Rocher du Diamant
Ste Anne
CANAL DE Ste LUCIE
Salines

Légende

- 🌿 Panoramas
- 🔴 Site ou curiosité
- 〰️ Plages
- ⌂ Hotels

25 to 26 degrees centigrade in February, to 28 or 29 degrees in August.

The rich soil seems to delight in being cultivated — bananas, sugar-cane, pineapples and a wide variety of tropical fruit and vegetables grow in abundance. The steep cliffs of the north and east, as well as the rocky headlands in the south, seem to exist simply to enhance the beauty of the magnificent beaches found in the deep bays and coves. And everywhere around the island "*la lèche hystérique de la mer*" — (A. Césaire), the ceaseless lapping of the coral sea — an immense reservoir for the greatest possible variety of tropical fishes.

Truly a privileged island!

history

The most ancient traces of inhabitation are attributed to the Arawaks "simple folk, kind, helpful to strangers, who would always have remained like this but for the unprecedented cruelties and insatiable greed of the Spanish which caused them to rise against their conquerors in order to throw off the unbearable yoke of tyranny." These relics are chiefly pottery of domestic or religious use, representing animals or caricatures of human faces.

It is believed that the Arawaks inhabited Martinique at the beginning of the Christian era.

8

They were driven out in about 180 AD by a volcanic eruption; there is evidence of them again from around the year 500 AD, until they finally disappeared in the tenth or eleventh century.

The first manifestation of Carribean genius seems to have been the invention of the polished stone axe. Pottery against axes, artisans against

Archeological research in the Antilles has unearthed evidence which confirms the successive civilizations of Amerindians. Many objects (see photos) are on display in the Museum of Fort-de-France.

warriors...the outcome was inevitable. The Arawaks were eliminated from the Lesser Antilles. However, it appears that the Carribeans killed the male Arawaks, whilst sparing the females in order to propagate the race: thus the first explorers were astonished to discover an ethnic group speaking three languages — an

everyday language, a separate one for the warriors, and yet another for the women. Christopher Columbus was amazed; Father Labat praised this strange phenomenon and proposed to European societies this example of a plurality of languages "because this extraordinary custom, though at first seeming strange, is not really

primitive: after considerable thought, it seems to me to be eminently sensible and very useful in restricting the superb feminine sex to their rightful role, and thus the respect that they owe to men."

The social organization and customs of the Carribean Indians are much better known to us than those of the Arawaks, for the British,

...panish and French chroniclers of the eighteenth century witnessed their resistance, and then their eventual disappearance at the hands of the invaders.

The Indians of Martinique attempted to resist the settlement by Europeans but were unable to struggle against firearms. Deeply committed to their own free way of life, they preferred to exile themselves or die, rather than assimilate and mix with the slaves, or to become subservient.

discovery of the antilles

While searching for the "Oriental Indies", Christopher Columbus discovered San Salvador in 1492, then Cuba and Haiti. He mapped and named part of the Lesser Antilles during a second voyage in 1493, and discovered Trinity on the third expedition. Martinique awaited his discovery in 1502 in the course of his fourth voyage.

He discovered Martinique but it is not sure that he actually went ashore: perhaps he was afraid of the snakes which drove away the Frenchman, Liénard de l'Olive, who arrived in 1635 to take possession of the island.

The inhabitants? "All are Indians. These people show no malice and are most unwarlike". Columbus believed and wrote that the island was peopled by a race of Amazonians. Many uncertainties surround the origin of the name of the island. Was it because the island abounded in flowers, or did he discover it on St. Martin's day? Certain writers claim that Martinique derives from Martinino, the island of women; others that it owes its name to Madinina, island of flowers, or to Martin, the patron saint of Christopher Columbus.

france

The Antilles, and in particular, Martinique, interested the Spanish only in that they were situated on what was known as the "spice route". France also coveted this region, but in order to avoid angering the Spanish monachy and the Pope, used devious methods to establish herself there.

In 1627, under the pretext of wishing to protect French trading interests against pirates, the king authorized all corsairs to trade freely in the Antilles. Pierre Belain d'Esnambuc, a nobleman from Brittany, staked his entire fortune on arming a ship, only to find himself almost ruined when his vessel was later wrecked on the shores of Saint-Christophe.

After France gained a foothold in the West Indies, the struggle for supremacy in the area became triangular — France, Spain and Great Britain. The history of the region during the following one and a half centuries reflects the vicissitudes of the armies of these three powers.

belain d'esnambuc

Because of its large area, Martinique was a much-coveted prize. From Saint-Christophe, Belain d'Esnambuc prepared his scheme to capture it. "Monsieur Belain d'Esnambuc, who should be regarded as the father and founder of all

The average size of the men rather larger than normal. They are all well-built and well-proportioned. The women are smaller than the men, quite solid in stature and plump: their eyes and hair are black, their faces round, mouths small, their teeth very white and, in general, they are gayer and more friendly than the men".

French possessions in the West Indies, meditated for a long time over the conquest of Martinique. He feared that the British were planning to take possession of the island and also that his glory might be eclipsed by his lieutenant, l'Olive, whom he had sent to conquer Guadeloupe; thus he decided to delay no longer". Initial contacts with the Carribean Indians were good, even cordial. The invaders declared that they were friends of the Indians "and these discussions were helped by the alcohol with which we plied them, and the presents which we gave, thus changing their hearts and causing them to promise to be friends of the new colony. They ceded all the area known as Basse-Terre and agreed to retreat to the Cabesterre".

The truce did not last long and there were soon incidents and sporadic fighting. The colonizers retreated into the fort of Saint-Pierre, while the Indians enlisted the aid of their allies from Dominique and other adjacent islands. However, luck was against them and they were forced to choose between death, exile or peaceful co-existence on the land which was allotted to them.

du parquet

After the death of Belain d'Esnambuc, his nephew, Dyel du Parquet, succeeded him as leader of the colony. In 1650, he bought Martinique from the Compagnie des Ameriques for 60,000 pounds sterling. The king appointed him Lieutenant-General in 1651.

At this time, the French Antilles were in the hands of four proprietors: Messrs. du Parquet, de Cesillac, Boisseret and Houel, as well as the Order of Malta.

The death of du Parquet in 1685 saw the final revolt of the Indians. They were defeated and forced to quit the island. In 1664 after the cession of the island by the children of du Parquet, the newly-formed Compagnie des Indes Occidentales became established by order of the king of France. Martinique remained a commercial estate until 1674 when the right to trade there was accorded to everyone. The king was represented by officers, governors and their superintendants, whose interests were not necessarily those of the inhabitants of the islands. An aristocracy, both demanding and anxious to retain its privileges, was at the origin of the uprisings of this period, the most famous of which was that of Gaoulé in 1717. This same nobility later prevented the French Revolution from spreading to the island.

Let us not look too far into the future, however. This battle of interests at the beginning of the eighteenth century is proof that the colony had by then become rich. But at what price?

slavery

The increasing prosperity of the island provoked labour shortages. The 200 colonists from Saint-Christophe multiplied, now numbering 6,000. Poor whites, indentured labourers who had agreed to work for three years under almost slave-like conditions to repay their passage from

France, were no longer sufficient to assure the development of the island's riches.

The colonists could not count either on the Indians who would not at any price accept to forego their liberty and thus destroy their social structure which was based upon hunting, fishing and bartering — activities which were not considered as work. They therefore asked to be allowed to introduce African

One of the statues in the "Place de la Savane" at Fort-de-France is of Nicolas Belain d'Esnambuc, a gentleman from Brittany, born in 1585, founder of one of the first French settlements in the Antilles, at Saint-Christophe. In 1635, he took possession of Martinique in the name of the Compagnie des Iles d'Amerique.

slaves. Slavery, though already practised by the Spanish, was forbidden in France, but Louis XIII finally authorized it for ostensible reasons which were very different from the real motives. "He finally gave in to the urgent solicitations which were made to him showing that this was an infallible means, the only one in fact, which could teach the worship of the true God to Africans, thus saving them from idolatry and forcing them to embrace the Christian religion until their death".

Religion to the rescue of commerce!

But conversion to Christianity was tough for these thousands of people torn brutally from their homeland, families and beliefs. After being either bought or kidnapped, the Africans were loaded on sailing ships, chained and thrown in the holds. If they survived the voyage, they were inspected like cattle and sold at the market. Besides being deprived of freedom and condemned to a life-time of hard labour, they were also subjected to corporal punishment which resulted at times in dreadful injuries.

In an attempt to restrict such cruelties, Colbert, in 1685, promulgated a law known as the *code noir*, which forbade all sanctions by slave-owners except for the birch or cane, bringing the right to judge and punish slaves under the jurisdiction of the law courts.

Despite a decree dated 15th April 1786, which imposed severe fines on masters who transgressed the law, the *code noir* existed in name only.

This ignominious situation continued in spite of wars and changes of regime.

The French Revolution abolished slavery in 1794, but this measure could not be implemented as Martinique threatened to become British rather than surrender to the French Republic. The Consul, Bonaparte, strongly supported slavery, influenced perhaps by his Creole wife, and by the fact that he did not wish to cede territory to the British. However, it needed a new revolution to finally wipe out this inhuman practice. Slavery was officially abolished by decree on the 27th April 1848. The instigator of these measures was a stubborn and headstrong man who made the liberation of slaves the cause of his life, and who is now venerated in Martinique both in songs and poems, as well as having many streets and public buildings named in his honour: Victor Schoelcher. Suddenly, 72,000 slaves found themselves free to leave their work on the sugar-cane plantations. Of course, it was necessary to find a replace-

ment labour force of Chinese and Indians until the growth of population, mechanization, and the economic crisis obviated the need for this.

During the period 1850 to 1900, the island's way of life took on a Republican character, and benefiting from the development of transport and improved techniques, kept pace with France and the rest of the world. The eruption of Mount Pelée on Saint-Pierre in 1902 was felt as a national catastrophe and, since then the Martiniquans have participated alongside the French during all world conflicts They enjoy the same representation as the French at the Chamber of Deputies and the Senate.

the present statute

Martinique has been a department of France since 1946, and comprises thirty-four local authorities, administered by a prefect. Three deputies and two senators represent the island. The mayors and their councils are elected by universal suffrage.

The main problems of Martinique nowadays are social and economic ones. The major effort is on finding employ- ment for the rapidly increasing population. A system of social security exists in Martinique, identical to that in France, but many people nevertheless emigrate to France in order to find work. Fluctuations in prices on the world market have caused a decline in the exploitation of the few traditional crops, thus forcing the authorities to try to diversify agriculture and assist the expansion of animal husbandry. The lack of mineral deposits and absence of cheap sources of energy make it difficult to promote industrialization. There is an urgent need to develop other activities which could provide a livelihood on the island; the most promising is probably tourism, but this calls for long-term planning.

The installation of the colonists' settlements, the elimination of the Carribean Indians, and the expansion of agriculture, augmented the island's need for labour. Whole shiploads of slaves were brought in from Africa and sold at local auctions for work on the plantations or for a master who had an absolute control over them, limited only in 1685, when the "Code Noir" was instigated by Colbert. Corporal punishment ranged from whipping to the wearing of chains (photo above shows slave chains displayed in the Museum at La Pagerie), or solitary confinement. The ruins of slave cells may be seen at Château Dubuc on the Caravelle Peninsular.
The statue of Victor Schoel- cher (1804-1893) in front of the Palais de Justice, Fort-de-France. Schoelcher was a liberal journalist who became the champion for the abolition of slavery after a voyage to the United States and the West Indies. When he was Under-Secretary of State to the Colonies, he promulgated a decree abolishing slavery in French colonies.

fort-de-france

"With great eagerness I plunged myself with devering curiosity into the streets in search of all the hidden delights they had to offer: The exotic markets, the musical voices, the women which Paul Eluard praised to me after his trip around the world as being the most beautiful creatures he had ever seen". (A. Breton).

This city, which Breton discovered in 1941 on his release from the internment camp at Lazaret, remains as he described it — big, ugly, but ever full of dazzling colors, intoxicating fragrances and beautiful women, carrying themselves so gracefully. Where the capital of Martinique stands today was nothing but a swamp in the thirteenth century. The only solid edifice which emerged from this marshy plain was Fort-Royal built by the Marquis of Baas, the first Governor-General of the French Antilles. This fortress, known today as Fort-Saint-Louis, owes its reputation of impregnability to the Dutch Admiral Ruitter who attacked it in vain in 1674.

It was a terrible assault, if one believes Father Labat —

When the Dutch Admiral tacked Martinique in 1674, is lump of land which we ready called Fort-Royal, onsisted of no more than a ouble layer of wooden stakes nclosing two elevated cannon latforms. The land on which ie city now stands was a vast vamp of reeds. There were nly a few temporary shacks hich, were used as stores. hese were filled with wine nd alcohol. When the sol-diers saw Ruitter's troops advancing, they pillaged the stores and drunk this liquor to such an extent that they were scarcely able to hold them-selves upright when the Commandant ordered them to attack".

Thus it seems the Dutch were driven off more by the powers of alcohol than by the strategic value of the fortress. Meanwhile, the Governor cited the excellent defenses of the fort when he chose it as the site for the installation of his headquarters. In 1682, Fort-Royal officially became the capital of Martinique. The swamp surrounding the stockade was drained and the Marquis de Blénac, then gover-nor of the island, drew up elaborate plans for the future city. Wide roads were built in the form of squares around the fort. The centre of the town still shows traces of this

Left: Aerial view of the bay of Fort-de-France. Between the mouths of the River Monsieur to the west and the River Madame to the east, is the Place de la Savane, the port and the center of the geometrically laid out town. Fort Saint-Louis is shown above.

early settlement: "a flat, spreading city, inert, made breathless by its geometric burden", wrote A. Césaire in his *Cahier d'un Retour au Pays Natal*.

fort-de-france

In 1793, Rochambeau named the town Fort Republique. Napoleon gave it its present name, Fort-de-France, on the 18th April 1802, but from 1815 to 1848, it was changed back again to Fort-Royal. Throughout all these changes of name, the locals continued to call it *Foyalais* (from "Fort-royalais", because of the absence of "r" in the creole language).

During the nineteenth century, the city was the victim of several disasters. An earthquake damaged many public buildings in 1839; a great fire ravaged the city in 1890, and in the following year it was devastated by a cyclone.

Fort-de-France increased greatly in importance after the eruption of Mount Pelée wiped the city of Saint-Pierre off the map at the beginning of this century.

Formerly only the administrative and military capital, Fort-de-France became the commercial, as well as intellectual and cultural, hub of the island. Today, the city has become isolated, with its mortar and brick replacing the natural flora and fauna of the remainder of the island. Buildings grow more rapidly than the vegetation as they sprout like mushrooms on the hills and on the new housing developments, which now shelter almost one third of the island's population.

la savane

This area of only five hectares is the heart of the city. Stretching along the sea-front, it is the nucleus to which all roads lead. As one leaves the town centre in the late after-

noon, one is rewarded by a magnificent view of the most majestic sunsets imaginable as the sun appears to descend slowly into the bay of Fort-de-France.

The bay and the port were known long before Fort-de-France became a city. To appreciate the vast expanse of the bay, one must go to Fort Desaix or La Moutte. But the port is close by, attached to the flanks of La Savane, the city centre, to which the passenger liners appear to tie their mooring lines, one porthole giving a view of the Carribean Sea and the other opening on to the harbor entrance through which the trading boats come and go today just as the smugglers' vessels did in earlier times.

The heyday of smugglers h *long since passed, but the sigh* *of sailing vessels moored t* *the quay of Fort-de-Fran.* *(above, left) brings to min* *the colorful past of th* *Antilles. The Saint-Lou* *cathedral, because of its met* *framework, is strong enoug* *to withstand cyclones an* *earthquakes. The Hotel de* *Ville (opp. page, above lef* *has the characteristic charm c* *administrative buildings* *French country towns. Th* *Victor Schoelcher Librar* *(opp. page, above right), bui* *for the Universal Exhibition c* *Paris in 1889, has 24,00* *books for the Foyalais t* *enjoy.*

carnival

Although Fort-de-France is the only town which pulsates with frenetic rhythm as exhausted crowds (*vidés*) swarm through the streets, Carnival is an event which involves almost the entire population of the island. In earlier times, Saint-Pierre was particularly renowned for the spectacle of its Carnival. In 1890 Louis Garraud wrote that "with the aid of a shortened shirt and a large

bonnet, the women like to disguise themselves as infants, while the men prefer to wear bright caps, short pants pulled in at the waist by a colored belt and a silk scarf thrown over their shoulders. The usual mask is a light open framework painted on the interior. No question of stifling masks or restricting fancy dress: everyone chooses the costumes which are the most convenient for enthusiastic

dancing". However, their disguises are certainly not mediocre or lacking in variation. The main idea is to render the dancer anonymous whilst conforming to the particular style and colour assigned to each day of the festivities.

Thus, for the election of the Carnival Queen on the Sunday evening, traditional costumes (scarves, madras, long dresses and finery) take pride of place, while on the day of Mardi Gras, the children dress up as little red imps. Armed with tridents, they follow a giant devil whose costume is studded with mirrors. Ash Wednesday is the day for black and white costumes, with everyone disguised as she-devils.

But, of course, the most important feature of the Carnival is the dancing!

"It is impossible for a European to believe that these people are capable of dancing non-stop from Saturday afternoon until Wednesday morning. Nevertheless, this happens each year from Shrove Sunday until Ash Wednesday." (Ph. Nourry).

Every year the Carnival dancers find new sources of inspiration to enrich the dances of previous years, and they fall in line, one behind the other, as they wind their way through the packed streets to a frenzied and incomparable rhythm.

The traditional Creole orches-

as comprise clarinets, drums, anjos or steel bands, but, if ese are not available, empty ottles and tins are used to ound out the rhythm of the ongs and dances.

his wild festival ends at idnight with the sacrifice of *aval* on a funeral pyre and

algré la vie à raide
aval pas quitté nous
algré la misère la
aval pas quitté nous.

opulation

artinique is an island (over) opulated by 300,000 inhabitnts on an area of 1,000 uare kilometers, equalling a ensity of 300 persons per uare kilometer. This populaon is divided into 90% egroes and mulattoes, 5% dians (coolies), 1% white eoles (*békés*), 3% pure rench, and 1% foreigners om diverse origins.

ixed blood

A fantastic people, amazing... ne is surrounded by people f mixed blood, the most eautiful mixture of races in e Antilles." (Lafcadio earn).

e first thing which imsses the reader of these gures is the extraordinary ixture of races which make the population of the land, and not one of these as indigenous. The original habitants, the Arawaks, were iven out by the Carribeans ho, in turn, were expelled by e Europeans. Although it

has become fashionable nowadays to speak of the ascendancy of the Carribeans, in fact, none of the present inhabitants descend from the original ethnic group of American Indians.

africa

de mon île lointaine
de mon île veilleuse
je vois l'Afrique multiple et une...
un peu a part mais à portée
du siècle comme un coeur de réserve. (A. Césaire)
Before becoming a *coeur de réserve*, Africa was a veritable reservoir of men, a prodigous mine of slaves.
Already in 1745, there were 60,000 slaves of African origin on the island for 16,000 white colonists and 1,700 free colored people. This gap is even more marked today. Ninety percent of the present population are descended from former African negroes and the importance of this colored ethnic element, which for a long time was chiefly only of demographic interest, has, in the past century, led the way in economic, political, social and cultural development. This evolution happened in successive phases: liberation of slaves in return for services rendered, permitting them to work for themselves (5 slaves freed in 1664, 4,500 in 1783 and 30,000 in 1838);

"This Africa which we accus of not having known how t protect its children, but whic at the same time retains i secret image of a paradise los In short, this swaying betwee a past which one wants t disown and a present whic we cannot accept because treats us badly". (A. Césaire).

the fact that the mixed-blood progeny from slaves and colonists were free;

the abolition of slavery which modified the economic structure;

the disaster of Saint-Pierre which wiped out a large number of the elite whites (*béké*);

the introduction of an increasing number of colored and negro people to education, and thus their accession to economic and political responsibility.

the whites

Apart from the indigenous Amerindians, white Europeans were the first occupants of Martinique. These adventurous pioneers, some from distinguished families, often braved great dangers and privations, both during their crossing the Atlantic from Europe, and after their arrival in this new land; but in only one century, their hard work and dedication had made the island a rich colony which they proudly defended, with weapons if necessary. Some renowned women also played a major role, amongst them Madame de Maintenon with Louis XIV, and Joséphine Tascher de La Pagerie with the Emperor Napoleon I. So jealously did the settlers guard their new homeland and way of life, that they threatened to hand the colony over to British rule rather than allow the French Revolution to take hold there.

The decline of this ruling class began with the abolition of slavery in 1848 and was greatly accelerated by the loss of many of their members in the disaster of Saint-Pierre in 1902. The white descendants (*békés*) of these pioneering families today number only several thousand, but they continue to defend their racial purity with the same intransigence as that which they

25

showed two centuries ago. Most metropolitan Frenchmen are employed in the Civil Service, which has been greatly expanded since Martinique became a department of France in 1946. With their own special sense of humour, the Creoles nickname these metropolitan frenchmen *Zoreilles* — we offer no comment!

the indians

Indians, Hindus, *"z'indiens"*

practised at religious gatherings.

island of women

Capresses droites et provocantes
bekées de lys et de langueur latière
chabines enjouées, marquées de soleil
coulies si fragiles et dont les traits sont purs
bel-ti négress fermes et saines mulâtresses aux grands yeux, souples. (G. Desportes)

all have that same indolent nonchalance, that same charm.

the market places

The markets are the favourite haunts of Martiniquan women: sellers or buyers, they animate their bargaining and disputes over even the smallest transaction with their musical creole tongue — for them, commerce is a game.

Trading in the vegetable markets begins in the very early morning. A powerful

or coolies — today they number about 20,000. Since the introduction of this race to Martinique between 1853 and 1884 to replace the liberated African slaves, these Indians have become entirely detached from their country of origin and have abandoned their mother tongue and former customs. The only traditions which have survived are a few ceremonial rites

Just as Christopher Columbus thought that he saw only women on the shores of Martinique, the visitor is often surprised by the prominent part that local women play in the life of the island.

Irrespective of racial origin or color of skin, all Martiniquan women, be they washerwomen of the River Capot or the elegant *"békés"* living admist the luxury of Didier, seem to

fragrance leads one to the stalls selling exotic spices; *bois d'Inde*, cloves, pepper, and the brightly colored red pimentoes. The market stalls are decorated with a huge variety of fruits and vegetables — guavas, pawpaws, bananas, custard apples, mangoes, avocado pears, potatoes, tapioca, watercress, cabbages, to name but a few. The fish market opens soon after

daylight when the fishermen return from their night's fishing, their picturesque canoes laden with the multi-colored produce of the Carribean Sea — tuna, tazars, bonito, and a variety of coral fishes.

the creole language

Cet enfant sera la honte de notre nom
cet enfant sera notre nom de Dieu
taisez-vous vous ai-je dit qu'il fallait parler francais
le français de France
le français des Français
le français français. (Léon Damas)

The many races thrown together in Martinique have given birth to a profoundly original population, which in turn has developed an equally original language — creole French.

Although more than ninety percent of Martiniquans have been to school and taught to speak French, for almost all of them, creole is the everyday language.

This rich tongue originated at Saint-Christophe as a result of the contacts between the Norman followers of Belain d'Esnambuc and the African slaves. It is characterized by a particular phoneticism, an imaginative vocabulary and an absence of syntax. It interprets and expresses perfectly the very soul of the people of Martinique for it has inherited their poetry and rhythm.

from fort-de-france to saint-pierre

This book is not intended as a substitute for the *Guide Bleu* which offers all the indispensable information for the tourist wishing to visit the island or plan his stay there. What we propose is to take the reader on a pictorial trip around this beautiful island. Every part of Martinique is worth visiting — from the extreme north of the island with its precipitous cliffs, to the rolling plains in the south; the Atlantic coast, as well as the other side bathed by the Carribean Sea; from the forests in the center of the island, to the fields of sugarcane on the coastal plain, not forgetting the banana plantations. And, everywhere, the scenery is enhanced by the smiling faces of the Martiniquans.

didier

At a distance of seven kilometers from Fort-de-France, the plateau of Didier dominates the city. In an atmosphere of quiet opulence, the vast mansions are concealed amidst immense gardens of carefully nurtured tropical vegetation — a reminder of the colonial heritage of the island. These family homes of the aristocracy of Martinique — the *béké* — have remained unchanged for more than a century. Most of them are built of wood, with their spacious rooms surrounded by a wide verandah. Huge trees, a hundred or more years old, shelter the gardens from the intense tropical sun, while lush flowers grow in orderly profusion. "Everywhere is order and beauty, luxury, tranquility and voluptuousness". Inside the homes, "the shining furniture, polished by the ages" is spaced far apart, lost in the vastness of the rooms. The furniture is made

precious local wood, and, [thou]gh copied from European [mo]dels, has, during the years, [de]veloped a character of its [ow]n — *style Martinique* — [inc]luding four-poster beds, [wa]rdrobes, settees and rocking [ch]airs.

[Ba]lata

[Sit]uated on the hills of Fort-[de]-France, the basilica of [Ba]lata offers the unreal [spe]ctacle of a castle lost in the [mi]ddle of a tropical forest. [Bu]ilt in 1928 along the lines [of] the Sacré-Coeur of [Mo]ntmartre, it is surrounded [by] the residential areas of [Fo]rt-de-France. This extra-[ord]inary building bears [wi]tness to the power of the [Ca]tholic church in Martinique. [Th]e ceremonies held there [off]er the local people an [ex]cuse to parade their finery.

le carbet

"The houses of the Antilles are called *carbets* — I have no idea whatsoever of the etymology of this word". (R.P. Labat).

In 1635, d'Esnambuc landed here before establishing his colony at Saint-Pierre. Here, also, Gauguin had his first taste of island life before continuing on to Tahiti, and then dying in the Marquesas. Le Carbet today is a village of fisherfolk, separated into two by a stream which rises in the peaks above the town. A beach bordered by coconut palms spreads its white sand for more than a kilometer. Fishermen place their fish to dry on the sand as they sit repairing their nets in this paradise. Canoes, under a shelter of palm fronds, await their next fishing trip.

The simple, unsophisticated church seems in harmony with the peaceful village. At the corner of the street, a woman displays the fruit of a day's fishing.

Amateur hikers may wish to leave the beach in order climb the peaks of Carb Piton Boucher (1050 m.), Grand Piton (1190 m.), Piton Dumauzé. The climbe rewarded with a magnific view over most of the isla and neighbouring Dominiq The vegetation on both si of the path makes the cli even more fulfilling: tropi forest, dense patches of a bu which the locals call "w olive" and then a sparser, t no less beautiful, kind vegetation at higher altitud The rivers surrounding

Carbet (Blanche River, Cadoré River, Monsieur River and Carbet River) are renowned for their *z'habitants* — a species of freshwater crayfish which are about the size of a small lobster, and which are considered to be one of the finest delicacies of Martiniquan gastronomy.

the winding road

A road from Fort-de-France to Morne Rouge was opened in the eighteenth century by the Jesuits. More a kind of track through the vegetation, rather than a road, like an open furrow between the immense bamboos, tree-ferns and lianas. The saturated air and constant humidity favours the tropical vegetation, thus described by M. Rufz: "It is here that one comes to the true realization of what is meant by primaeval forests. A wierd light, greenish, bluish at times, like the clarity of the moon at midnight, confuses the real and imaginary shapes. A foul dampness seems to exude from everything and a smell of death hangs heavily in the stillness which is not really silence... one is inspired by this mysterious and primitive eeriness".

morne rouge

This small village, situated at 450 meters altitude between the peaks of Carbet and Mount Pelée, was completely annihilated by a second eruption of the volcano on the 30th August 1902, just two months after the destruction of Saint-Pierre.

A shrine erected on the mountain slope commemorates the 30,000 victims of the Saint-Pierre disaster and also the 1,500 who disappeared from Morne-Rouge and Ajoupa-Bouillon.

saint-pierre

"Les montagnes trembleront comme une dent prise au davier". (A. Césaire)
The eighth day of May 1902,

36

ven-fifty in the morning. A gantic explosion caused the rth to shudder and the sea boil. "An enormous mass of re, stone and mud hurled self on the city, covering it, loking it and setting it lame, then continuing to roll iwards into the sea, reading in all directions and expanding like a mountain of re and ashes." In less than ve minutes, the city of iint-Pierre and its surroundings were completely vastated — an area of sixty quare kilometers. Thirty ousand inhabitants perished, ther asphyxiated or burned o death, the governor of the iland and the mayor of the ty included. Thus the capital f Martinique, and the onomic and cultural center f the island, was obliterated om the map.

he carribeans curse

ere there any among the 0,000 victims of that terrible ay in May 1902 who emembered the curse put pon them by the last of the arribeans in 1658? After a olent battle, many of the rviving Indians gathered on le edge of a precipice, gouged ut their eyes and hurled lemselves to their death on le rocks below, preferring is to subservience. They died hilst threatening that the lountain of fire would wreak leir revenge.

he Administration paid little eed to this Carribean curse, or to the signs which

preceded the disaster. The "mountain of fire" was, however, no stranger. In 1792, the first eruption of Mount Pelée made the authorities aware of the need for *surveillance*. A Commission of Inquiry was formed in 1851: its members concluded with perspicacity — "To sum up, Mount Pelée seems to be nothing more than one extra curiosity to add to the natural history of our Martinique. When the weather is calm and clear, passengers on ships arriving from France can see from afar this long, undulating column of white smoke rising towards the sky, a picturesque decoration for the island and a fitting complement to the majesty of our venerable Mount Pelée".

In April 1901, this "extra curiosity which added to the natural history of Martinique" became a problem. Signs of the awakening of the long dormant volcano became more and more frequent and of increasing violence.

But the machinery of an orderly government cannot accept the disorder of Nature. An election was due to take place, and there was no question of the voters abandoning the city.

Orders were given that reports from the Administration must "henceforth have a reassuring tone". A commission name by the governor enlisted th aid of a professor of natur sciences who claimed "it is m opinion that Mount Pelé presents no greater danger t Saint-Pierre than Mour Vesuvius does to Naples' That day of May, voting da the day of mourning, the da of reckoning... Mount Pelé buried the city of Saint-Pierr under a heap of molten larv and ashes.

In 1635, Belain d'Esnambu landed at the mouth of th River Roxelane, and afte concluding an agreement wit the Carribean Indians "h established his headquartte near the river mouth, buildin

ount Pelée dominates the
wn of Saint-Pierre, a
enacing background to the
autiful bay. "Mountain of
re" of the Carribeans, it is
outed to have had its first
mors in the 10th or 11th
ntury. Some carvings dating
om the 18th century (opp.
ge) prove that the ex-
osions, although infrequent,
re nevertheless spectacular
d terrifying.

e photograph below, taken
March 1903, shows the
tent of the devastation of
e town. One can see a shaft
larva at the tip of the
mmit of Mount Pelée,
rced upwards by the
ntinual underground
essure.

Martinique. — 3.   La Montagne Pelée

a fortress of palissades which he armed with several cannons. He soon constructed houses to lodge his colony and, when he had assured their safety and comfort, he cleared a large patch of land and planted manioca, peas, potatoes, cotton and tobacco". (R.P. Labat).

Thus was born the prosperity which spread from Saint-Pierre to all Martinique and throughout the entire Antilles.

Even though Fort-Royal became the residence of governors, and later the administrative and military centre of the island, Saint-Pierre remained the capital for economic, commercial and cultural activities.

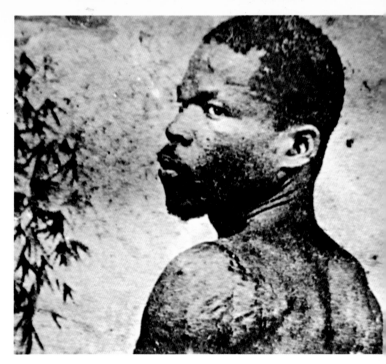

Sylbaris (above), condemned and imprisoned in a thick-walled cell which was protected by the Morne Abel, was the sole survivor of the eruption in 1902. The stairway (lower right) is all that remains of the splendid theater of Saint-Pierre, which was modelled on the same lines as the famed theater at Bordeaux.

1902, Saint-Pierre was
eater than ever before, with
anks, newspapers, printing
resses, rum distilleries, a
otanical garden and, above
l, its theatre which was an
xact replica of that of
ordeaux and the pride of the
ty.

he sole survivor

he sole witness to the
bliteration of this proud city
as a prisoner named Sylbaris,
cked in the solitary confine-
ent cell of the jail, which
as situated at the foot of
forne Abel and was thus
rotected by this small
illock.

ocked in the dark confine-

ment of his cell, Sylbaris could not, of course, understand what was causing the intense heat during those five awful minutes of the disaster. For years afterwards, this incredibly fortunate survivor was displayed as a curiosity throughout the world by the Barnum circus. A few lucky sailors and passengers aboard the ship "Roddam" also

Rouge and Ajoupa-Bouillon. Today, seventy years later, Saint-Pierre still bears the sinister marks and scars of its torture. The town lives again, rebuilt around the remnants of its prestigious past: the ruins of the former college, the cemetery, the theatre, the former cell of Sylbaris and the ruins of the church of the fort of Roxelane.

Martinique. The Dutch Jew driven out from Braz perfected the technique making sugar in Martiniq The founding of several sug refineries at Bordeaux a Nantes orientated Martiniq towards a monoculture sugar-cane, and the great r in demand for sugar result in increased productio which, in turn, created t need for a vast labour force thus the introduction slavery.

sugar cane in econo

Sugar-cane — the instigator slavery and the source of t fortunes amassed by so mai whites and creoles, is today regression. Victor Sabl Deputy for Martinique, h reminded us of the evolutic of this cultivation. "From t moment that we chose t option of higher salaries jus fied by rising prices and a improved standard of livin without implementi measures to finance ne techniques and greater pr ductivity, any amate fortune-teller could forese the effects and name a tin when, unless the governme intervened, the sugar-ca industry would begin downhill slide".

From 92,000 tons in 196 sugar production has falle slowly but constantly and, spite of government measures taken in 1966 to ha this decline, has never bee more than 30,000 tons i recent years. This decline

escaped, even though "two-thirds of the ships in the port, after a sinister cracking of all their woodwork, had their masts and poops smashed, cut off and carried away, and they went to the bottom within minutes, some by the bows and others stern first".

The eruption continued sporadically until the month of August, when the final convulsion of the volcano on the thirtieth day of that month was equally as severe as the first, destroying Morne

sugar cane

Endemic in the Far East, sugar-cane was first introduced into the Mediterranean basin and to parts of the Arab world, where people rapidly acquired a taste for it. It was then planted in the Canary Islands, and from there to Haiti in 1506. It was not until the year 1640 that Jean Aubert introduced it to Guadeloupe, and ten years later, du Parquet brought it to

roduction is due partly to ariations in prices on the orld market which renders e position of the industry ery precarious, and also ecause of the tendency of bourers to now seek easier id better paid employment. owever, despite the decrease sugar production, the indus-y still continues to be one of e significant features of the artiniquan way of life.

he harvest

he flowering of the cane, lled the "arrows" takes ace from February to May, id the harvest mobilizes out 40,000 people. Cane antations cover 8,000 ectares of tilled land on the land, though the geographi-l allotment of the farms is ot very precise. In spite of creased mechanization, the orkers' movements have mained the same for two

---

am the one who goes
irefoot
1 the rough stones of
mented roads
ith a hoe on my shoulder
id my cane-knife swinging
am the big negro worker
am he who is seen bent over
the sugar-cane plantations
listening with sweat
the glaring sun, my back
ent and my arms bare
y back is broken
nd my hands clenched on
e hoe
am the big black worker

(G. Desportes)

centuries. The cutters slice off the bushy tops and lay the stalks of cane in piles which are then bound into neat bundles by the *amarreusses* and stacked in large heaps, which are later loaded on to carts, trucks or wagons for transportation to the mills.

sugar

On arrival at the mill, the cane is unloaded and passed through powerful revolving cylinders of the crushers to extract the raw juices, which are later purified and crystallized. Most of this raw sugar is shipped to the refineries in Bordeaux or Marseilles for the final processing.

After being passed through the mill a second time, the juice that still remains in the cane can be fermented, though not crystallized. The stalks are thus put through a third time, and the resulting juice is fermented to make molasses, and this, in turn, is fermented and distilled into a pure alcohol called "industrial rum".

This rum, which is sold throughout Europe and the United States, bears no resemblance to "agricultural rum" which is obtained from pure sugar cane juice. The latter is filtered, fermented and distilled to produce a superior alcohol known as *grappe blanche*. There is as much difference between these two types of rum as exists between *taffia* — a local brew — and real rum.

rum

Rum — the ritual drink of the island — is omnipresent at all hours of the day and all days of the year. Local tradition has it that the body of a newborn baby should be rubbed with rum, while, at the

end of a rum-filled life, a gla
of this ubiquitous alcohol
poured into his mouth c
death. Each morning
pétépié or "take-off" —
large glass of rum mixed wi
absinthe and the juice c
various plants, ensures that th
new day will be a pleasurab
one.

In earlier times each estate he
its own sugar-mill and ru
distillery. Nowadays there a
only a few of these distilleri
left, but they keep to the o
traditions and make hig
quality rum. The measuring c
the rum (below right) is dor
with great care; then it is age
in enormous containers to gi
it color, strength and taste.

And finally, at any hour of the day or night, the *ti-punch*, for which the essential is "the desire and a real enthusiasm for this drink. And for the preparation — everything is at hand. Pure cane syrup, either white or matured rum — each drinker has his preferred brand — a green lime and a cube of ice, plus a long-handled spoon to stir the mixture. Special care is taken in measuring the ingredients, the quantities of each being a matter of personal taste, varying according to the time of day, circumstances and one's mood". (G. Raspail)

Recipe for a Martiniquan Punch:
1/5 pure cane sugar syrup
4/5 rum (either brown or white)
a zest of green lime and a cube of ice.

the north of the island

Although not a noted tourist region, the extreme north of Martinique, bordered by the Carribean Sea, offers a scenic beauty which has few equals. The west coast lives under the menace, if only because of the sinister souvenirs which still profoundly mark the landscape, of the eruptions of Mount Pelée: streams of volcanic larva strewn over the enormous rocks, beds of torrential rivers, precipices, almost inaccessible beaches, a sombre vegetation of moss and ferns.

le prêcheur

The road from Saint-Pierre to Le Prêcheur crosses the River Séche and the River Chaude, and then continues past the Tombeau des Caraibes, the

precipice from which the last Indians threw themselve when pursued by th colonists; later, it traverses th site of the former village c Saint-Philomène, which wa destroyed by the eruption c 1902.

Ten kilometers north c Saint-Pierre, one arrives at village which owes its name - Le Prêcheur — to a now nor existent islet whose shap resembled that of a preache in his pulpit. The celebrate Father Duterte, author c

"Histoire Generale de Antilles", was once in charg of this parish, one of th earliest on the island.

History has left a few othe traces: a plaque commemc rates the activities of d Parquet, another reminds u that Madame de Maintenor spent part of her childhoo here. Born François d'Aubigné, she was th daughter of Constan d'Aubigné and grand-daughte of d'Agrippa. Her fathe obtained a concession of lan in this region after his releas from prison in France an attempted to establish tobacco plantation. Seve years after his arrival in 1638 the enterprise proved a failure and he left Martinique Françoise cherished fon memories of her creol childhood and later, a Madame de Maintenon, sh used her influence with th king to plead the cause of th Antilles.

the anses (coves) of the north

Further north, between Le Prêcheur and Grand-Rivière, there is a small but passable road which traverses the region called "Abymes" (a French name describing its steep slopes), and skirts the Anse Belleville before coming to an end at Anse Ceron: here the sea is often rough, the beach is beautiful, and one can see the picturesque Ilet de la Perle in the distance.

Beyond Anse Ceron, the road is no more than a track 15 kilometers long leading to Grand-Rivière, and it is bordered on one side by anses which are accessible only by sea.

the north coast

"At the end of the dawn, this most essential country, restored to my inmost greed, not with widespread tenderness, but with the tormented sensuality of a cluster of hills like full breasts with an occasional palm tree, fruit of a hardy seed, the leaping exaltations of torrents and, from Trinité to Grand-Rivière, the hysterical lapping of the sea". (A. Césaire)

Grande-Rivière: the return of the "gommiers" at dusk, sale of fish on the beach, and Dominique in the distance.

grand-riviere

The village of Grand-Rivière, situated at the extremity of the island, facing out towards Dominique, seems to be constantly battered by the sea. The 1500 inhabitants divide their time between cultivating the hills which dominate the village, and fishing in the open sea. They are renowned as intrepid sailors and for their fishing skills. They voyage far out in the open sea in search of tuna, dorado and striped mackerel, so far in fact that Martinique is lost to sight —

Below: a Hindu temple (koilou), a simple shack decorated with small statuettes painted in bright colors, situated between Lorrain and Basse-Point.
Right: from Basse-Pointe one can see the coast of Dominique.

locals call this "going to miquelon."

macouba

"To give full justice to the inhabitants of this parish, I must assure you that I have never before seen people show so much kindness to a priest, or who have done this with a better grace". (R.P. Labat)
The numerous visitors to the village of Macouba since the days of Father Labat affirm that such hospitality is not only reserved for the clergy! But everything in the village bears witness to the past: a church flanked by buttresses, a cemetery which seems to be suspended above the ocean, this small township of 2,000 people which has retained its original Carribean name (Macouba is the name of a species of fish). Macouba became famous in the eighteenth century for the

quality of its *petun* — tobacco.

z'indiens

The prosperity of this region in the seventeenth and eighteenth centuries brought about a great demand for labour. After the abolition of slavery, many unsuccessful attempts were made to introduce a low paid labour force of Chinese, Amanite, Lebanese and European origin. From 1854 until 1885, imported Indian workers filled the gap. They were indentured for a period of five years and, after this term, they had the right to remain on the island if they chose not to return to their homeland. Of those who remained in Martinique and Guadeloupe, a minority was assimilated into the local population, while others formed separate groups or communities.

The Martiniquans refer to them as *z'indiens* or *coulies*; this latter term was originally derogatory — since they replaced the former slaves as plantation workers, the Indians were considered to be inferior. Their numbers now total about 15,000 in Martinique (the majority are of the Dravidian race), and they can be distinguished from the Martiniquans less by the color of their skin than by their slender bodies, their fine faces, rather aquiline noses, and their sleek black hair. Most of these Indians have

embraced the catholic religion, but they have also kept their temples — simple shacks of wood and corrugated iron — and the religious traditions of their original homeland. At Easter, a sacrifice takes place: the drums (sheep-skins stretched over an iron frame) are heated, and the priest, in a trance, is hoisted on the blade of a sword held by two assistants; this sword is then used to sever the heads of sacrificial chickens and sheep. All their prayers are said in a language which is no longer understood, neither by the priest nor his followers, and the ceremony exists as nothing more than a homage to their ancestors, and as a much sought-after tourist attraction.

basse-pointe

A small commune where Aimé Césaire was born in 1913: an old church and a small Hindu

temple bear witness to the coexistence of the two religions. In the past, Basse-Pointe was of some commercial importance, producing cocoa, sugar and coffee. Children there are renowned as skilful surfers and can be seen practising this sport on the Atlantic waves.

ajoupa-bouillon

This small village, whose name is of Carribean origin (*Ajoupa* means a cabin) is an important center for the cultivation of bananas and pineapples.

It is also from here that excursions leave for Saut-Babin. This waterfall of about ten meters in height is accessible first by car and then by a small tow-path which descends around the gorges of the River Capot. The numerous other rivers which follow the slopes of Mount

The mansion of Pecoul (preceding page) was one of the finest houses of the eighteenth century. This region of the island, one of the richest, was the first to be exploited. The ruins of the houses of the former supervisors, the distillery, the mill and the workers' huts of the old settlements of Capot, Chalvet and Leyritz are striking reminders of the past. Left: to reach the Babin precipice from Ajoupa-Bouillon, one must leave the car and cross the fragile footbridges which span the rivers.

Pelée — the Poquet, Roche, Macouba and Lagarde Rivers — are the rendezvous of the washerwomen. Their work progresses joyfully between bursts of laughter, and the banks and nearby bushes are festooned with the multi-colored garments which are spread upon them for a few hours to dry.

the atlantic coast

Situated between Ajoupa-Bouillon and Marigot, the market-town of Lorrain was founded in the eighteenth century, and for many years remained the most prosperous town of this fertile region on the eastern slopes of Mount Pelée.

The numerous ruins of abandoned houses testify to the former prosperity of this town. Some large plantations in the area nowadays produce bananas, pineapples and sugar-cane.

The former name of the locality was Grande-Anse, after the name of its bay. The sea here is always rough and the beach is often battered by the great swells of the Atlantic.

In the vicinity, the ruins of Capot (sugar mill and slave cells) and those of the Pécoul mansion which dates from the eighteenth century, make this region one of the richest souvenirs of a glorious past.

In the picturesque old village

of Marigot, P. Pinchon discovered important archeological evidence of early Carribean civilization. The coast here is beautiful but fully exposed to the wind and ocean swells.

sainte marie

Saint-Marie, with its population of 20,000, is the second most important commune of the island. It is situated on an archeological site dating from the time of the Arawaks, and stretches for about two kilometers. The town faces an islet which, at low tide, is joined by a sandspit to the mainland. The sheltered bay is much more protected from the Atlantic Ocean than Marigot or Lorrain. The principal activities are fishing and the cultivation of sugarcane; one of the largest sugar mills of the island is foun here.

le fond saint jacque

Just to the north of the villag is the monastery of Fonc Saint-Jacques, founded by th Dominican Order in 1654 o land donated by Madame d Parquet after the final ex pulsion of the Amerindian from the region of Capesterre This monastery is famou

ecause it was renovated and
in by the energetic Father
abat after finding it in a
ilapidated state in 1694.
roud of his achievement, he
rote "one could really see
ie difference when I left it in
705". Of this cherished
uilding, all that remains
)day are the ruins of the
onfessional and the chapel.
he former mill, however, has
ow been restored.

morne des esses

Above Saint-Marie, the people
of the area known as Morne-
des-Esses have conserved the
traditions of basket-making
which are handed down from
generation to generation. In
the seventeenth century, this
cane-work was used both for
their own household needs —
baskets, mats etc., and also as
a form of currency for trading
with the colonists. Today it is
perhaps the most popular of
handicrafts for souvenir-
hunting tourists visiting
Martinique.

trinité

At the head of the harbor,
between Saint-Marie and the
nearby island of Caravelle, the
township of Trinité, which in
the eighteenth century was an

administrative center and headquarters of one of the King's lieutenants with his four regiments of militia, now has a population of 9,500 and is a sub-prefecture of the island. Its former prosperity, due to its trading activities as well as its proximity to Fort-Royal, was thus described by a traveller: "The port of Trinité is a deep inlet protected by a headland. This trading post has increased in importance because of the considerable quantities of cocoa, sugar and cotton which are produced hereabouts, especially in the hills; many merchants and vessels are attracted here". Trading schooners no longer call at Trinité, but fishermen and here in the late afternoon with their colorful catches to supply the local market — a spectacle well worth seeing.

the caravelle peninsular

A peninsular of about 15 kilometers in length juts out into the Atlantic Ocean — *la presqu'île de la Caravelle.* The shores are deeply indented, hacked out, rather than cut, by the incessant battering of the wind and sea; here, homesick wanderers are often reminded of the coast of Brittany!

On the very tip of the peninsular, between Point Diable and Point Caracoli, the meteorological station stands alone and solitary, braving the fury of the Atlantic.

tartane

Situated between Trinité and Point Diable, the fishing hamlet of Tartane is the furthermost inhabited spot. There is a splendid beach bordered with coconut palms, and one may sample here all the varied products of the sea — innumerable varieties of tropical fishes and especially succulent sea-urchins. Because of the abundance of fish, the peninsular is a paradise for underwater spearfishermen.

the dubuc

The Caravelle peninsular — a deserted wilderness on the northern face — is adorned on the southern side by the splendid bays of Calion and Tresor. The latter bay is renowned above all for the ruins of the former settlement of a family named Dubuc de la Rivery, who played an active role in the history of the the presqu'île to British sovereignty. By a quirk of fate, the only surviving relic of this once powerful family domain are the slave cells sheep pens, the dam and an old mill.

la sultane validé

But the most legendary figur of the Dubuc de la River family was without doubt th young Aimée, who was bor at Fort-Royal in 1775 c 1776. History reserved for he

The Caravelle peninsular, "Presqu'île de la Caravelle", the furthest point of the island, jutting out into the Atlantic: desolate and lashed by high winds, this is a paradise for underwater fishermen. Numerous tropical fishes of all species inhabit its coral-filled waters.

Right: carrying sharp spikes, children setting off in search of white sea-urchins (chadrons).

island; in particular, in the affair known as "du Gaoulé" of 1717, which symbolised the opposition of the colonists to the misdeeds and abuses of power of government officials. One member of the family, Louis François Dubuc, was one of the principal leaders of the movement which was instrumental in preventing the spread of the French Revolution to Martinique. During eight years he actually ceded

a fate somewhat like that o Rose Tascher de la Pagerie, fo under totally different circun stances and in quite anothe world, she also played the rol of an empress.

At the age of nine years, sh was sent to school in France a convent of the Vistandin order. Five years later, becaus of fears for her safety durin the French Revolution, sh left Nantes, bound for Sain Pierre. But the ship neve

reached its destination. After being shipwrecked in the Bay of Biscay, Aimée and her nursemaid, Zorah, were rescued by a Spanish vessel which was subsequently captured on its way to Majorca by pirates from the Barbary coast: the passengers were taken as slaves to Algiers. Aimée was bought by the Dey of Algiers and given as a present to the Sultan of Constantinople, becoming, so the story goes, his favorite wife and the step-mother (or perhaps the mother) of the future Sultan Mahomed II. She told her story to a Capucine monk who was called to her bedside to minister the last rites in 1817, but, in fear of reprisals, the tale was not revealed until 1826.

le robert

"The cul-de-sac Le Robert is the most beautiful natural harbor imaginable".
This was the description given in 1694 by Father Labat when he arrived there to establish the parish of Le Robert. A former township where the last Amerindians lived in the eighteenth century, this area is well worth a visit to see the beauty of the bay and its picturesque cemetery. On the third Sunday of September each year, a nautical festival is held here, with the people from the nearby islets of Madame, Ramville and Loup-Garoup also taking part.

le francois

This village is renowned in Martinique because it has one of the best teams for racing sailing yawls. Le François was also the birthplace of General Brière de l'Isle who, according to Larousse "after distinguishing himself at Bazeilles in 1870, was made Governor of Senegal in 1877: he later returned to Tonkin, where he commanded a brigade, and was made Commander-in-Chief of the area in 1884. He recaptured Tuyen-Quan, but after the loss of Langson, was obliged to retreat to the delta region. Recalled to France, he ended his career as Inspector

Left: Le Robert, its bay dotted with islets, the church, and a "gommier" with rectangular sail.
Center: the town of Le François with a funeral service in progress (above). In the country districts, these ceremonies still follow the old creole tradition which was most likely inherited from African "griots". An orator stands outside the house and recounts episodes from the life of the deceased, interspersing his speech with chanting. The audience responds (les titime - bois sec) and joins in the recital. Then rum is distributed to moisten their tongues and alleviate their grief.

of the Marine". The destiny o
this celebrated warrio
contrasts strangely with th
serenity of the agricultura
village of his birth.

South of Le François, on
must hire a *gommier* to visi
the islets of Thierry, Oscar
Long and Fregate so that on
may contemplate the cul-de
sac of Fregate in all its beauty

and the rhythm of steel band
The *vidés* (exhausted partici
ticipants) dance their wa
through the streets to th
sound of drums. Everything
song and dance and "it is n
only their mouths, but the
hands, their feet, the
buttocks, their sexual orga
and indeed their whole bein
which melt into sound, voi
and rhythm", (A. Césaire).

the creole soul

There exists a certa
ambiguity in this term whi
derives perhaps from t
contradictory ways in whi
poets and writers ha
employed it. For some, it is
synonym of exoticness, t
invitation to travel and t
search for an idyllic utop
where "there exists only ord
and beauty, tranquillity a
voluptuousness".

For others the Creole so
means the search for
identity and is "the angui
which a colored person fee
for the plight of his kin". (
Breton). This was the quest
Aimé Césaire, poet a
politician; likewise of Fran
Fanon, psychiatrist, exile

*In the southern part of t
island, the scenery is bo
varied and contrasting: t
white sand beaches of L
Salines (above), the escar
ments along the coast and
Devil's Table (opposite), a.
the petrified forest (righ
where there are only rocl
cactus and sparse grasses to
found.*

because of his ardent anti-colonialism. But, above all, the Creole soul is the soul of a people. Its origin stems from a mixture as precise as that required for the preparation of a perfect rum punch — a background of common language, sun and nonchalance, rum, and the mentality which results from living on an island "which further accentuates the differences in general behavior of newcomers from France and the Martiniquans". (Ph. Nourry). Add to this the love of dancing — mix all these factors, stir them well, and the result... the charm of the Antilles.

the south of the island

The southern part of Martinique, though less mountainous than the north, offers at least an equal diversity of scenery: large bays, beaches of fine sand, lonely hills in the far south, green fields of sugarcane, the precipices of Point d'Enfer — all combine to make the meridional coast a fitting complement to that of the north.

table du diable

The small islet of Cabrit facing the coast is separated by a narrow channel. At the eastern extremity, a rocky promontory jutting out into the sea bears the striking name of Devil's Table. It looks like a

detached chunk of the island adrift in the Saint-Lucie channel.

the petrified forest

After crossing the saltpans of Les Salines, one comes to a geological curiosity, the petrified forest. This desert of silicified wood, the only live vegetation being cactus, was probably originally a forest which was mummified by a volcanic eruption: the atmosphere of desolation which it exudes seems bewitched.

le marin

At the south of the western slopes of the island, tucked away at the end of a cul-de-sac bearing the same name, is the town of Le Marin with its 6,000 inhabitants.

This former garrison post of one of the king's platoons was always coveted by the English, who pillaged it in 1693; they were repulsed during subsequent attacks in 1762 and 1808.

The cul-de-sac forms a veritable inland lake joined to the sea by a narrow passage which is difficult to cross.

The church, built in the eighteenth century Jesuit style, with its separate bell-tower, is certainly the most beautiful on the island.

A bay cut into deep inlets like a labrynth, the church (right), one of the oldest on the island, and a Martiniquan woman (opp.) wearing traditional costume.

the southern carribean coast

The economy of Martinique rests on three hopes: the development and diversification of agriculture, industrialization, and the expansion of the tourist industry.

tourism

Martinique has the great advantage of being situated in a region which naturally lends itself to tourism, and of being able to offer a particular quality of service with a personal touch. All parts of the Antilles enjoy a constantly warm temperature. They are easily accessible from all continents by regular air lines or by charter, while those few lovers of long voyages may travel there by ship. And, in this gigantic mosaic of islands, Martinique is blessed with a unique diversity of scenery and an exceptionally equable climate. Added to this is the fact that, as an aftermath of history, although Martinique is so close to the American continent, France has endowed the island with a language, way of life and a charm which differs greatly from the rest of the West Indies.

Besides these favorable conditions generously bestowed by Nature, the Administration has now shown a real desire to develop the infrastructure which is indispensable to the long-term development of tourism. A total of 1,198 hotel rooms already exist, and there are plans to build another 1,800 before the end of the Sixth Plan in 1974. Future planning also provides for the creation of a nature reserve in order to protect and display the flora and fauna of the island, the installation of a golf-course of international standard on Trois-Ilets, and the building of ports for pleasure boats.

The beach, the extraordinary clarity of its water, and the installation of the Club Méditerranée (left) makes Saint-Anne one of the most attractive tourist resorts of Martinique.
The village (right), with its old wooden houses, has retained the charm of former times.

sainte anne

The Club Méditerranée, whic has for many years been o of the leading organizatio catering for tourists seekir out-of-the-ordinary holidays Europe, and is now expandir to the United States, h. established a vacation comple at Pointe du Marin, near to tl very attractive town of Sain Anne, which has 3,00 inhabitants. Situated in the f south of the island, it has a the natural conditior required for the developmer of a high-class tourist resort; beautiful beach of fine san bordered by coconut palm clear water, a picturesqu town with a shady villag square, and a church built c sandstone.

sainte luce

Saint-Luce is a village of 3,000 inhabitants whose principal activity is fishing in the open sea and in the Saint-Lucie channel. Like most of the settlements in this region, it was destroyed by the English in 1693, and later ravaged by the cyclone of 1817.

During the festival which marks the day of their patron saint, there are canoe and sailing races which attract many enthusiastic spectators.

canoe races

The most famous canoe racing teams come from the villages of Le Robert, Le François and Le Vauclin, as these people are without doubt the most experienced in handling the vessels in the rough condition of the Atlantic Ocean.

It was the Carribean Indian who taught the Martiniquan the sciences of seamanship and navigation. Their tradition vessels were thus described in 1842 by A. Dessalles: "The double-ended canoes in which they travel from one island to another are about nine feet in length by four and a half feet wide.

Several holes are drilled in each side and a kind of rope basket, like a hammock, is fashioned by passing cord through these holes: this serves to store their goods or belongings during the voyages" These storage racks like long, sausage-shaped nets suspended above the sea allowed more room for passengers and helped to stabilize the fragile vessel which were frequently over turned in the rough sea. *Gommiers* have a single square sail supported by a diagonal sprit.

Most of these canoes are hollowed out from a single log of the local tree known as *gommier* — a species of gum tree. At the time of Father Labat, all such trees were reserved for the making of canoes. The scarcity of these trees and the labour involved in making such canoes, has resulted in their virtual disappearance and replacement by *yoles*, which are common type of racing skiffs.

oles

These planked vessels are built from local timbers which are carefully selected, and which are also becoming rare. The construction, and later the maintainence, is very carefully carried out in order to coax the maximum possible speed from these prestigious racing boats which are transported from one village to another to compete in the sailing races held as part of the festivities in onour of the different patron saints.

The naming of these boats seems to be a contest to find the most original: "Revenge to Traitors", "Guardian Angel", "Evinrude", "Air France", "Jealous Ones to the Rear", "Boeing", and "Concorde", to name but a few!

oles are equipped with either one or two masts and, for their size, carry an extraordinarily large area of sail.

But the most important factor is the crew, for it takes a good deal of practice to master the skills required to sail these fast craft in the competitions which attract so many fervent supporters.

The "gommier" has many uses: as a comfortable chair in which to dream of one's youth (above left), under full sail during a race (below left), or right) it can be loaded on a truck to go and take up the challenge given by a neighbouring village.

All the villages enter into the sailing races with keen enthusiasm. The most renowned crews come from the Atlantic coast, though all Martiniquans are excellent sailors. The enormous sail areas render the vessels unstable in strong winds, and wooden planks are thus fixed to the sides so that the crews can counterbalance the sails and keep the vessels upright. Nowadays it is no longer permitted to throw a crew member overboard in order to lighten the boat in calm conditions.

cock fighting

Cock-fighting is as popular in the Antilles as horse-racing is in France or bullfighting in Spain. A fighting cock is specially reared and trained for this purpose: "Splendid birds, pure bred, highly trained, strutting about each morning in the open air and deprived of the sight of a madame-hen for eight days before the combat, given every encouragement, fed on the best steak, their plumage multicolored, striking and of perfect size, their crests trimmed, their rumps and the feet feathered, their skin red (for white skin indicates weakness of muscles), their wings trimmed symetrically to enable quick leaps and dangerous thrusts of their feet... thus killing with their murderous spurs, either natural or artificial ones made of stainless steel, depending upon the type of combat. Doping is recommended, and each cock breeder has his own secret formula". (J. Raspail). Inherited from the Greeks and the Romans, and introduced to the Antilles by the Spanish, cock-fighting is now a firmly-established sport. It provides an excuse for men to meet and lose themselves in formidable bouts of oratory; the spectacle involves more than just the actual cock-fights — the pit (where the contest is held) is filled to bursting point with gamblers, and there is great excitement as the owners present their birds for weighing and the bets are laid before the combat begins.

The two birds eye one another and feint like boxers, but if this lasts too long, it provokes recriminations by the spectators. Though the real fighting should be with the

spurs, the cocks also use their beaks. Each thrust has a special term: to the pectoral is known as *coup d'blanc* (thrust of white), to the head, *coup d'cérébral* (brain thrust). If a cock loses too much blood, the wounds are rubbed with green limes to stop the bleeding, but the bloody combat continues until one of them lies dead on the sand of the pit.

other combats

In 1635, snakes caused Monsieur de l'Olive to decide against disembarking on arrival at Martinique, though the intrepid d'Esnambuc landed and settled there later that same year.

The reputation that Martinique had as an island of snakes was certainly justified, and caused the colonists to be on their guard against this danger at all times. It was not until 1883 that a solution was found, with the introduction of the mongoose, the celebrated enemy of snakes, to the island. So well have the mongeese accomplished their task, that there are almost no snakes left there: perhaps they have been even too efficient, for it will now probably be necessary to attempt the elimination of the mongeese which attack other domesticated animals.

The fascinating spectacle of a combat between a mongoose and one or several snakes is sometimes organized at Fort-de-France. The mongoose is usually the winner: if it manages to take the head of the snake in its mouth, it shakes its opponent, holding onto its grip until the snake dies. Occasionally the mongoose is the loser, if it is bitten on a part of its body which it is unable to lick.

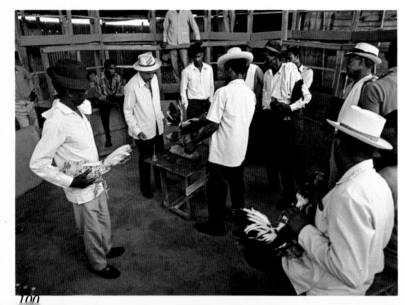

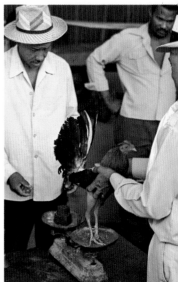

le diamant

Diamond Rock serves as a homing ground for an infinite number of birds, amongst them, wood-pigeons which make their nests there. Access to the Rock is difficult, but does not prevent us from visiting there occasionally during the season when the young wood-pigeons are fat and excellent to eat (De Rochefort, 18th century).

The small village which stretches along the seashore owes its name to the diamond-shaped rock. The majestic Morne Larcher slopes right down to the edge of the sea, joining a magnificent beach

pigeons: two hundred were installed on the Rock, where they remained for eighteen months. The presence of this garrison, only a few hundred meters off the French-held coast, proved intolerable for the French Admiral de Villeneuve, who drove off the English in the following year.

the "du gaoule" incident

The ruins of the O'Mallane estate, a few kilometers from Diamond Rock were the scene of the mutiny known as "du Gaoulé".

In 1716, the exigencies of the Governor — de la Varenne, and his assistant — Ricouart,

goes, they invited the Governor and his assistant to a banquet at the residence of O'Mallane. The Duke of Saint Simon takes up the tale in his memoirs: "There happened in Martinique a revolt so secretly organized and so singularly well-planned, that it can be said to be without equal. Varenne was Administrator of our island, and Ricouart his assistant. They lived in style in Martinique and contrived to look after their personal interests far more than those of the inhabitants, whom they treated very unjustly.

Repeated complaints by the settlers invariably fell upon deaf ears. Thoroughly

some four kilometers in length. This region, inhabited since 1664, was the cause of much rivalry between the French and the English. In 1804, English soldiers there outnumbered the wood-

102

sparked off a rebellion of the plantation owners, who were angered by the attempts of the government to limit the production and the number of sugar mills. After planning the revolt in secret, so the story

Left: the strange Diamond Rock.
Above: tombstones in the cemetery decorated with lambis shells.
Opp. page: the white church dominated by Morne Larcher.

disgusted by the tyranny and villaging of these officials, and seeing no hope of justice by conventional means, they resolved to take matters into their own hands. Never before had these colonists worked together with such accord. The two officials were taken by surprise one morning after a great banquet at the D'Mallane estate and handed of the strong motivation which lay behind their illegal exploit. Indeed, there was great admiration for the secrecy and moderation with which it was executed".

the anses

From Diamond Rock to Trois-Ilets, exquisite bays of unequalled beauty have been

fishing

"Fishing with cast-nets, with frond torches at night, even with their bare hands; the Carribeans are experts at the game. Our negroes have learned from them and are now as competent as their teachers". (R.P. Labat).

The Martiniquans owe a great deal to the original indigenous

their papers and personal effects neatly packed and sealed. They were then loaded in a well-equipped vessel which set sail immediately.

The action of these colonists could not, of course, be approved, amidst the surprise which it caused, but neither were they condemned because hollowed out of the Martiniquan coast by the Carribean Sea. The splendid beaches of white sand bordered by swaying coconut palms provide idyllic conditions for fishermen with their long seine nets — a familiar and very picturesque scene. Carribeans, from whom they learned many things about fishing and the sea, thus helping them to adapt to their new surroundings, whilst eking out a living from their catches. About 3,000 people, chiefly in the centers of Grand-Rivière, Belle-fontaine, Fond-Lahaye, Vauclin and Robert, now depend entirely upon fishing for their livelihood, while numerous others are part-time fishermen, or operate on a subsistence level.

the marine fauna

"The fishes are as decorative as peacocks; blue, yellow, red — colored in a thousand different ways". (Christopher Columbus).

One of the main attractions of Martinique is found in the seas which surround it. The plants and animals of the coral bottoms and reefs offer an unforgettable spectacle — an enormous variety of colors and shapes of the great diversity of species: starfish, sea-cucumbers, both black sea urchins and white, trumpet shells (which seamen still use for signalling), clams, small octopus, flying-fish, sting-ray, multi-hued dorados, box-fish, crayfish (*z'homards*) and fortunately, very few sharks

Fishing techniques

The habits and habitats of the many species of fish and the variety of natural conditions, the availability of many natural materials such as canes and lianas etc. with which the fishing gear is made — all this, plus the ingenuity of the local inhabitants, has led to the development of a wide array of traps and other traditional fishing gear. Cane or wire netting traps are used in relatively shallow water: they are baited with the remains of crabs, fish and crayfish or crushed sea-urchins. A rope from the trap to a buoy marks the place where they are set. The traps are hauled up every two days and often contain crayfish, many species of reef fish, and, occasionally, moray eels.

On the deeper reefs, only a few kilometers offshore, handlines are used to catch such fish as coral snappers,

rock cods etc., while fisher
men who troll lines wit
artificial lures as far as 3
kilometers off the coast, some
times return laden wit
bonito, tazaar (striped gian
mackerel), dorado and tuna
One of the most productiv
fishing methods is sein
netting, using immense nets a
much as 500 meters long an
30 meters deep. These net
represent a considerabl
investment and often belon
to a group of people wh
finance the operation an
appoint a "seine master" t
take charge of the actua
fishing operations. Seines ar

A beach, canoes and fisherme
at a village named Ans
d'Arlets, situated betwee.
Grande-Anse and Petite-Anse

set only in bays or regions free of coral and rocks which could damage the net. When a school of fish is sighted, one end of the net is held ashore and the net boat is rowed out with great speed, thus spreading the net in an immense semi-circle around the fish. It requires a good deal of manpower to haul these heavy seines, and the local people often join in the operation in exchange for part of the catch. Fish are often driven into the net by slapping the surface with paddles or by banging stones together underwater.

The same net is also sometimes used as a ring net or gill net to encircle schools of fish in the open sea, usually with good results.

Molluscs and sea-urchins are also gathered by the local fishermen. One of the most popular shells for eating is the Lambis, a type of Stromb which has firm, white flesh. These are gathered by skindivers and the shells are then broken to extract the fleshy parts.

The delicious local white-spined variety of sea-urchins known as *chadrons* are gathered with a long-handled spike, and are always cleaned in the area where they are collected.

grand anse

The magnificent beach of this picturesque fishing hamlet is ideal for seine netting. Gauguin is said to have been
110

inspired by the beauty he saw here.

anse d'arlet

This village is named in honor of a Carribean chief called Arlet, and a brother of the Chief Pilote mentioned earlier. It was sacked by the English in 1792.

The many canoes lined up on the shady beach indicate that

a lot of fishermen operate from here. A semi-circle of hills in the background make the village look like an immense amphitheater. With its small white church, this is one of the most charming of all Martiniquan villages.

On the other side of the bay of Fort-de-France, facing the town, la pointe du Bout, jutting out into the Carribean Sea, makes this the largest and most protected harbor in Martinique.

The splendid scenery, beautiful beach and the

proximity of Fort-de-France from which Point du Bout is accessible both by car and by boat, combine to make this one of the most popular and rapidly developing tourist areas. The local hotels have already installed a veritable tourist complex comprising tennis courts, golf courses, swimming pools, restaurants, night clubs and a marina.

Fortunately, the natural beauty of Point du Bout has not suffered from this new development: the installations appear to be part of the natural landscape, virtually unseen along the length of the white sand beach, as they blend harmoniously with the luxuriant tangle of the tropical vegetation.

trois ilets

This small village owes its present name to the fact that it is situated on a plateau giving a splendid view of the

ree islets in the bay of Fort-
e-France. In former times it
as known as the *cul-de-sac à
ches* (or cow-field). In
350, Napoleon ordered that
e then neglected church,
ting from the eighteenth
ntury, be restored in
emory of his Empress
osephine. Indeed, much of
e town seems to be a
emorial to the Creole girl

*he La Pagerie estate (former-
· called Petite Guinée)
overed more than 500
ectares. The only remaining
uildings have been trans-
ormed into a museum in
emory of the young Creole
rl who became Empress of
rance.*

*he village of Trois Ilets: the
hurch,· with its triangular
onton and wooden steeple,
here Joseph Tascher de la
agerie married Rose-Claire
es Vergers de Sannois and
here Josephine was baptised.*

who, by winning the heart of General Bonaparte, became the First Lady of France.

A few kilometers along from Trois-Ilets, nestled at the bottom of a lush green valley, is the estate of La Pagerie, where the Empress Josephine entered the world on the 23rd June 1763. Born to Joseph Gaspard Tascher de La Pagerie and Rose Claire des Vergers de Sannois, she was baptised Marie-Joseph Rose on the 27th July 1763. The first ten years of her childhood were spent happily in the tranquility of the estate, which was then known as La Petite Guinee. She was then sent to boarding-school at Fort-Royal. Two events of importance in her early years were firstly the hurricane which ravaged the buildings of the estate in 1776 and forced the family to take refuge in lodgings which we hastily improvised in t church, and secondly, in 177 when an old negro fortun teller, named Euphemis Davi predicted that someday sl would become "more than queen".

In 1779, at the age of sixtee years, while in France, sl married Alexandre, son of tl Marquis de Beauharnais, former Governor-General the Leeward Islands. Tw children, Eugène and Horten (who was later to marry Loui brother of Napoleon I, th becoming the mother Napoleon III), were born this union which brougl unhappiness to both partie In 1788, Josephine decided return to Martinique, whe she installed herself in specially built house on tl family estate. She was Fort-Royal when the troubl provoked by the Frenc Revolution commenced. Sl embarked on the first ship France and arrived there ju in time to see her husban General Alexandre Beauharnais, mount tl scaffold on the 21st Jul 1794, and she narrow escaped a similar fate.

Six years later, on the 9t March, she married anothe general, Napoleon Bonapart as yet unknown, and thus sl entered into the history France. But, nine years late on the 16th December 180 since she had not produce him a son and heir, Napoleo obtained permission from th

Pope to divorce her. She die
on the 29th May 1814 at L
Malmaison, without havin
seen again her beloved home
land.

the museum

La Pagerie is now owned b
Doctor Rose Rosette, who h:
renovated the property an
arranged with loving care tt
small objects and earl
mementoes of the childhoo
of the Empress Josephine.
A former two-roomed house
one room was the kitchen, an
the other the bedroom c
Madame de la Pagerie – it h:
now been arranged as tt
actual museum which is ope
to the public. All the usu.
paraphenalia belonging to c
Creole Martiniquan family c
the period are on displa
pottery, local basketwor!
kitchen utensils, iron colla
and fetters of slaves etc. The
are also many origin:
documents and souvenirs c
the infant Marie-Joseph Ro:
– certificates of birth an
baptism, her first cot, an
many reminders of tt
Napoleonic era. The house i
which Josephine de Beauha
nais lived on her return t
Martinique in 1788 sti
stands; other relics include a
old bridge, the ruins of tt
windmill, sugar mill and stor
rooms.
A few kilometers on fro:
Trois – Ilets, one comes to
pottery and brick-making ki!
which carries on the traditio
al artisanal production c

bricks, jars, water pitchers and other pottery, all of which sells well nowadays in Fort-de-France.

When the Europeans introduced the potter's wheel to the Antilles, the ancient methods used by the Arawaks and the Indians soon became obsolete. Though the early inhabitants used only primitive techniques, they managed to make all their necessary utensils. The Arawaks used a method known as *trois pans* (three pan system) which consisted of applying the hand-mixed clay in three successive layers. The Amerindians employed another system which entailed winding a long ribbon of clay in a spiral until the vessel took on the desired shape. A plaque fixed above the entrance to the pottery is inscribed *ici, le travail transforme la terre en or* (here, earth is made into gold).

plants and animals

Unlike the fauna of Mart[i]nique, which is relatively poo[r] the flora is characterized b[y] an extraordinary abundanc[e] variety and luxuriance. What [is] even more astonishing is th[e] fact that the majority of th[e] vegetation is not endemic, bu[t] has resulted from a series [of] chance happenings, and some times from introduction b[y] man.

From the point of view [of] vegetation, the island [of] Martinique can be generall[y] divided into three fairl[y] distinct zones: the coast[al] plain, the agricultural zon[e] and the forests.

the agricultural resources

Agriculture in Martinique [is] based essentially on th[e] intensive culture of thre[e] crops: sugar-cane, bananas an[d] pineapples. Sugar-cane ha[s] played a very important ro[le] in the history of the islan[d]

because it was responsible fo
the development and pro
sperity of the area during th
eighteenth century and
perhaps even more importan
was also the reason for th
introduction of slave
Although its heyday has lon
since passed, fields of suga
cane clothe the gentle slope
of the windward coast an
many of the alluvial plain
while providing employmen
for 40,000 workers in th
height of the season.

The climatic and soil co
ditions in many parts o
Martinique are also ideal fo
the cultivation of banana
This fruit was first introduce
to Saint-Dominique as early
1516 by Father Thomas o
Barlonga, and soon spread t
all parts of the West India
Intensive cultivation in th
French Antilles dates fro
about 1930, and there h
recently been considerab
expansion of the plantatio
as a result of the introductic
of specially constructe
"banana boats" which tran
port the fruit to France
freezer holds. There are no
10,000 hectares of bana
plantations with an estimate
20 million plants in Martin
que, producing 200,000 to
of bananas per year. From th
time of planting the you
suckers, it takes only 9 to
months for them to bear fru
The bunches are harveste
while the bananas are st
green and are kept in co
storage until arrival in Franc

where they are artificially ripened before being sold.

Pineapples constitute the third most important agricultural crop, after sugar-cane and bananas, and they are mostly destined for the export market. The fruit is harvested between May and July, the majority of this work being done by seasonal workers.

The present trend of agriculture in Martinique is to diversify as much as possible and to develop the culture of small

crops and fruits which can be exported. Many crops such as aubergines, cucumbers and green peppers can thus be imported into France as out-of-season produce. The exportation of exotic fruits such as guavas, mangoes and coconuts takes place throughout most of the year.

In 1965, the production from small-scale market gardens was only 5,000 tons, but this should increase to 30,000 tons by 1975. For the past few years the farmers, in collaboration with the authorities, have been trying to overcome the precariousness of an agricultural economy based upon only three principal products – sugar, bananas and pineapples, which are necessarily subject to the vicissitudes of world price fluctuations.

In addition, every effort is being made to increase the yield from the 20,000 hectares

of land which are at present used for grazing and dairy farming. Modern methods of intensive farming on smaller plots of land are rapidly being adopted.

The main emphasis is on crops which can be exported in an effort to rectify the balance of payments currently operating at a deficit of more than 70 percent. Partly because of investment in heavy machinery and equipment, and also because most of the food, clothing and luxury articles are imported, the value of exports nowadays is equivalent to only 28 percent of that of imports.

terrestial fauna

The luxuriant Martiniquan vegetation harbors a relatively poor fauna. Very few species have been introduced; nor have many endemic ones disappeared. Most of the animals found today existed before the arrival of the Europeans.

In the towns, one seldom comes across more than the small green lizard (anoli), the large cockroach, which inhabits most houses, a few insects, the most notable of which is a species of firefly and a tiny, rose-colored frog. In the countryside, there are still a few snakes which have escaped the predatory mongoose, but these are rare and present no danger. The most common birds are the colibri, a species of humming

rd which is often seen flitt-
g around the hibiscus and
ougainvillea, and the small
cali, a canary — the whistler
f the mountains. The giant
oads or *buffo,* which were
robably introduced to con-
ol cane beetles, are now very
ommon. Along the seashore,
ere are several species of
abs: *tourlourou, mal z'oreil-*
s and *c'est ma faute;* the
tter is so called because it
ems to beat its chest with its
onormally large claw. All the
sual insects of tropical areas

*he most common flowers of
'artinique are the hibiscus
eft), bougainvillia (opp.),
'lamanda (below) and
nthurium (below right).*

are found — mosquitoes, bees, ants, dragonflies (*zing-zing*) and crickets etc.

ducos

Before arriving at Fort-de-France, one passes through Ducos, a small village which was once called by the poetic name of *Terre au chat* (land of cats). In 1855, it was given

its present name, in honor of Jean-Etienne Théodore Ducos, the Minister for the Navy and the Colonies during the Second Empire. The buildings are relatively new (the church was built in 1901) for the old village, dating from about 1670, was completely destroy-ed by a cyclone in 1891.

le lamentin

From Ducos, the road winds through vast sugar-cane plant-ations on its way to Le Lamentin, passing by the largest sugar-mill of Martini-

que, the Lareinty.

This town owes its name to the manatée, a marine mammal which was common along this part of the coast in the eighteenth century. "The Spanish named it *monate* or *manati,* meaning a fish with hands, and we call it Lamantin. It seems to me that it should be called a "sea-cow"

for its face, its mamma glands, and its way of givi birth and suckling the your all bear a resemblance to cow". (R.P. Labat).

In this same area where the beasts once swam and graz on sea-grasses, there is now oil refinery and the int national airport of Fort-d France.

martiniquan folklor

The zombies, mama, are th real
Very real, very real, my ch
There are zombies whi resemble a big woman
There are others which can k with a glance,
so deadly is their hideousne
There are others who, inste of a head, have a blank ma without mouth, without no without eyes, without an thing
If the zombies talk to you n children, never reply.

In spite of the fact that almc all Martiniquans are Christia the beliefs inherited from the African ancestors remain ve much alive. Although magic not as prevalent in Martiniq as it is in Haiti, where tl *voodoo* of Dahomian orig is practised, it is nevertheli very common.

The *quimboiseur* is the int mediary between the occ forces and the world of tl living: "he" heals, gives advi and intervenes to arran matters and settle disputes, well as using his influence call on the supernatu

into which nails are driv
parcels of bones, feath
quantities of earth and o
ingredients, the mixture
which is as secret as its po
is terrifying. The magic sp
are called *quimbois:* it is
that the word derives from
days of Father Labat, w
when treating the sick, g
them a potion saying *t
bois* (here, drink!). Bes
the practice of sorcery,
cosmology of the Antille
peopled by spirits who h
come back from the land
the dead to survey
threaten the living.

The *mamas de l'eau* (wo
of the water) are witc
whom all sailors fear; the
diabes kill people; the *do
rape young girls; the *g
blesses* are ghost-like wo
dressed in white, who le
behind them a trail of de
tation; and *gagés* are pec
possessed by the devil, tr
formed into animals. Fina
there are the zombies wh
represent all the spirits of
and those of the night.

glossary of creole terms

Acra: doughnut, fritter
Ajoupa: cabin or hut
Amarreuse: woman who ties the bundles of sugar-cane at harvest time
Anoli: small, green lizard
Bakoua: fisherman's hat
Béké: white creole
Béké-goyave: poor white Martiniquan, living in the countryside
Blaff: fish cooked in spiced water
Cabri-bois: insect which is noisy at night
Cabrouet: ox-cart
Calalou: thick "gumbo" soup made with okra pods and spices
Câpre, Câpresse: person of mixed blood, three-quarters being negro blood
Carbet: former communal building of Carribean Indians
Caye: coral reef (word of Spanish origin)
Chabin, Chabine: light-colored person with fine features and
128
frizzy hair
Chadron: sea-urchin
Colibri: humming-bird
Colombo: highly-spiced curry sauce with saffron
Coui: bowl made of half a calabash
Coulie: coolie, or Indian chappé-coulie — mixed negro and Indian
Créole: white person born in the Antilles
Da: nursemaid, nanny
Décollage: rum drunk first thing in the morning before eating
Féroce: highly-spiced dish of cod, avocado pear and tapioca flour
Gommier: gum-tree, or dugout canoe made from this tree
Habitation: residence of a colonist, or estate
Homard (z'homard): lobster, crayfish
Laghia: dance which mimics a combat
Lambis: edible mollusc: the
shell also serves as a siren o fog-horn for sailors
Morne: hill, mound
Pat'en pot: soup made wit mutton and fine herbs
Pitt: arena for cockfights
Quimbois: magic spell usuall administered as beverage
Ravet: large variety of cock roach
Séancier: person who is both sorcier and healer
Soudon: shellfish resembling clam
Soupe z'habitant: vegetabl soup
Thé: infusion of local herbs
Ti bo: to kiss
Touloulou: small red crab
Trace: path
Tray: serving tray carried o the heads of local women
Vidé: popular parade ac companied by songs
Z'habitant: kind of freshwate crayfish
Zombi: phantom, ghost

martinique

Photography by **Bernard Hermann**
The English text was adapted from the French original by **William Reed**